CLINICAL PATHOPHYSIOLOGY

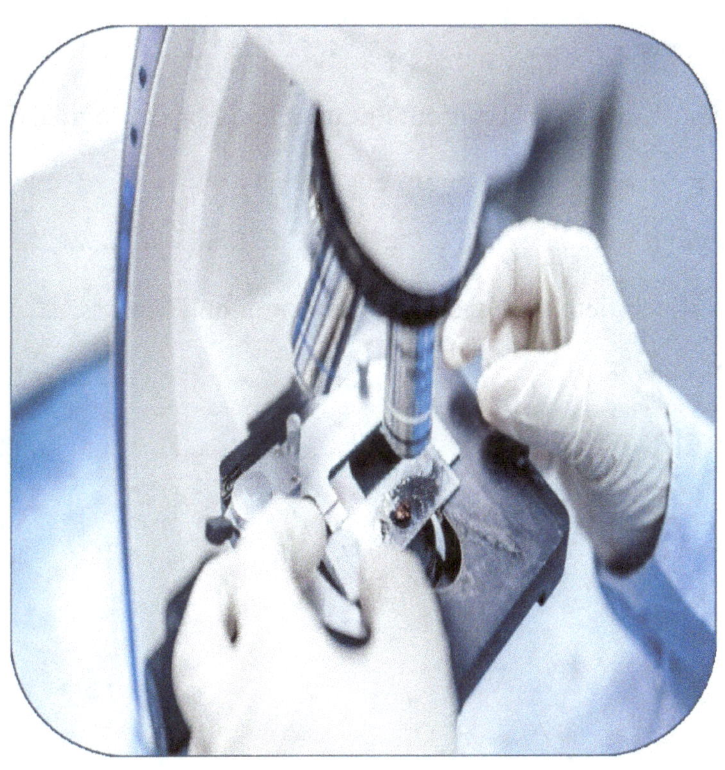

TABLE OF CONTENTS

INTRODUCTION

In the dynamic world of healthcare, staying informed about the intricacies of disease processes is vital. For healthcare providers, whether you're a respiratory therapist, doctor, or nurse—having a deep understanding of clinical pathophysiology is essential to making sound clinical decisions. This book, Mastering Clinical Pathophysiology: A Comprehensive Guide for Healthcare Providers, was crafted with the goal of equipping you with the knowledge needed to navigate the complexities of disease mechanisms. From understanding the body's physiological responses to illness to interpreting diagnostic tools like X-rays and determining the best treatment plans, this guide serves as a practical and comprehensive resource.

Clinical pathophysiology is the study of how disease affects normal biological functions. It bridges the gap between understanding the cause of a disease and identifying its signs, symptoms, and treatment options. For healthcare providers, mastering this knowledge is a crucial skill. It allows you to anticipate how various pathophysiological changes manifest, make accurate diagnoses, and provide appropriate care. Moreover, learning to interpret X-rays, spot abnormalities, and understand physiological signs are vital aspects of a provider's responsibility.

Whether you are an experienced clinician looking to refresh your knowledge or a healthcare student eager to deepen your understanding, this book serves as a valuable resource to enhance your practice. As we explore the critical aspects of clinical pathophysiology, my hope is that this guide not only informs but also inspires you to remain curious and engaged in your continued learning.

LESSON: UNDERSTANDING CLINICAL PATHOPHYSIOLOGY: THE FOUNDATION OF DISEASE

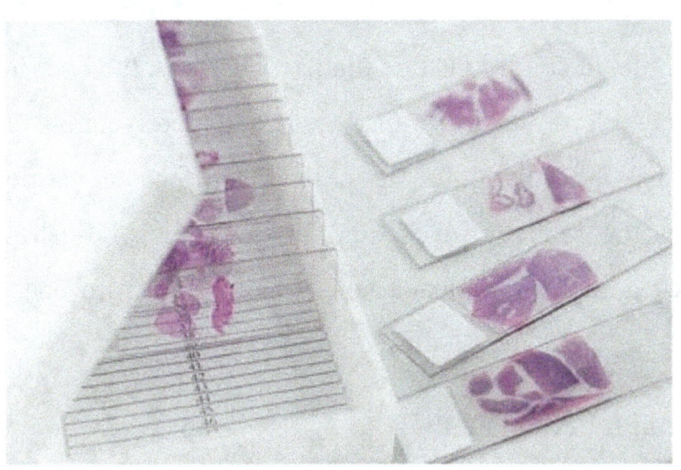

Clinical pathophysiology sits at the heart of healthcare practice, influencing every decision healthcare providers make when diagnosing, treating, and managing diseases. It is the study of how normal physiological processes in the body are altered by disease, injury, or infection. As healthcare providers, understanding this foundation is essential to becoming proficient in recognizing early disease signs and providing the most effective care.

The Concept of Homeostasis and Disease

At the core of pathophysiology lies the concept of homeostasis, the body's ability to maintain a stable internal environment despite external changes. Homeostasis involves various physiological systems, including the cardiovascular, respiratory, endocrine, and nervous systems, working together to maintain balance. Disease occurs when these systems fail to adapt to stressors, leading to a breakdown in homeostasis. Understanding how diseases disrupt homeostasis provides critical insights into their manifestations.

For example, in conditions like diabetes mellitus, the body's inability to regulate blood sugar levels leads to hyperglycemia, disrupting homeostasis. This disruption has cascading effects on various organs, including the kidneys, eyes, and blood vessels, illustrating how systemic pathophysiological changes can occur from one disrupted process.

Etiology and Pathogenesis

Two key concepts in pathophysiology are etiology and pathogenesis. Etiology refers to the cause of disease, which may be genetic, infectious, environmental, or a combination of factors. Pathogenesis describes how the disease develops and progresses in the body. A solid understanding of these concepts helps healthcare providers determine the origin and trajectory of a disease, guiding diagnosis and treatment strategies.

Let's take a common condition like pneumonia, where the etiology may be a bacterial, viral, or fungal infection. The pathogenesis involves the invasion of the respiratory system, leading to inflammation and fluid accumulation in the lungs. This, in turn, results in impaired gas exchange, contributing to the clinical manifestations such as coughing, shortness of breath, and fever.

Cellular Responses to Injury

The body's cells respond to injury in various ways, including atrophy, hypertrophy, hyperplasia, metaplasia, and dysplasia. These cellular changes are central to understanding the progression of disease. For instance, when the heart muscle undergoes hypertrophy in response to increased workload, as seen in hypertension, this can lead to heart failure if the underlying cause of the increased demand is not addressed.

Inflammation and Immune Response

Inflammation is the body's primary defense mechanism in response to injury or infection. The process of inflammation involves a complex interaction of immune cells, signaling molecules, and the circulatory system. Understanding the mechanisms of inflammation, including acute and chronic inflammation, is vital for recognizing how the body reacts to pathogens, trauma, or other harmful stimuli.

In chronic diseases such as rheumatoid arthritis, persistent inflammation leads to tissue damage and joint deformity, highlighting the importance of controlling inflammatory processes in preventing long-term damage.

Clinical Relevance of Pathophysiology

The study of clinical pathophysiology is not just theoretical—it directly influences patient care. For healthcare providers, recognizing how diseases alter normal physiology allows for accurate diagnosis, anticipation of complications, and timely interventions. This knowledge serves as the basis for interpreting diagnostic tests, identifying the right treatment approach, and monitoring patient progress.

MODULE TWO

LESSON: THE PHYSIOLOGICAL AND CLINICAL SIGNS OF DISEASE

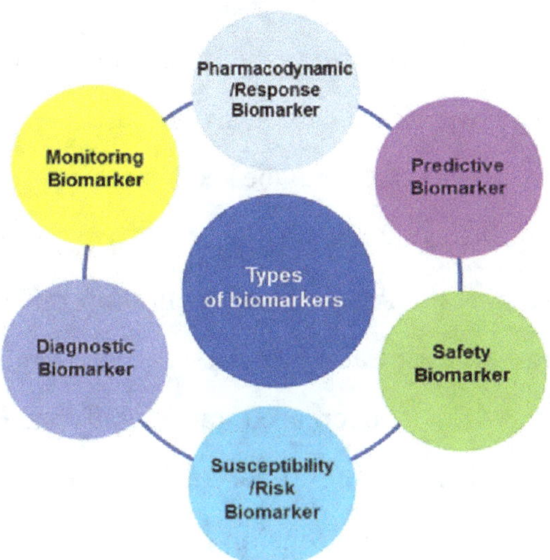

Recognizing the physiological and clinical signs of disease is essential for healthcare providers, as it allows them to identify the presence and progression of illnesses early on. A deep understanding of these signs not only enhances diagnostic accuracy but also facilitates effective patient management and treatment planning. In this lesson, we will explore the major physiological and clinical signs associated with various diseases, focusing on how to interpret them within the context of pathophysiology.

Vital Signs: The Cornerstones of Clinical Evaluation

Vital signs, heart rate, respiratory rate, blood pressure, temperature, and oxygen saturation—are the first indicators of a patient's health status. These are crucial parameters that reflect the body's immediate physiological response to stress, illness, or injury. When these signs deviate from normal ranges, they provide early clues about underlying conditions.

- Heart Rate: Tachycardia (increased heart rate) may indicate fever, hypovolemia, or heart failure, while bradycardia (decreased heart rate) may be seen in athletes or during certain heart conditions like heart block.

- Respiratory Rate: An elevated respiratory rate (tachypnea) can be a sign of respiratory distress, pneumonia, or metabolic acidosis, while a decreased rate (bradypnea) may suggest opioid overdose or central nervous system depression.

- Blood Pressure: Hypertension can indicate cardiovascular or renal issues, while hypotension may suggest shock, dehydration, or heart failure.

- Temperature: Fever often signals infection or inflammation, whereas hypothermia can occur in cases of exposure, sepsis, or metabolic disturbances.

- Oxygen Saturation: Low oxygen saturation (hypoxemia) suggests impaired respiratory or circulatory function, such as in chronic obstructive pulmonary disease (COPD) or pulmonary embolism.

Understanding how vital signs correlate with physiological changes is fundamental in clinical pathophysiology. For example, a patient presenting with tachycardia and hypotension may be in shock, while bradypnea and altered mental status may indicate impending respiratory failure.

Clinical Signs of Respiratory Diseases

Respiratory conditions, such as asthma, pneumonia, or COPD, are common in clinical practice. Recognizing their clinical manifestations can help guide timely interventions.

- Dyspnea (shortness of breath): This is a hallmark sign of respiratory distress, often seen in conditions such as asthma, heart failure, or pulmonary embolism. Pathophysiologically, dyspnea results from impaired gas exchange or increased respiratory effort due to airway obstruction or lung damage.
- Wheezing: A high-pitched sound heard during breathing, wheezing often indicates airway constriction, as in asthma or bronchitis. Pathophysiologically, it results from turbulent airflow through narrowed bronchi or bronchioles.
- Cough: Productive coughs suggest infection, such as in pneumonia or bronchitis, while dry coughs may indicate asthma, viral infections, or irritant exposure.
- Cyanosis: This blue discoloration of the skin and mucous membranes is caused by low oxygen levels in the blood, reflecting severe hypoxemia, as seen in advanced COPD or severe pneumonia.

A deeper understanding of the pathophysiology behind these signs helps healthcare providers determine the severity of respiratory diseases and the appropriate treatment. For instance, a patient presenting with dyspnea, wheezing, and cyanosis may have an acute asthma exacerbation requiring bronchodilator therapy and oxygen supplementation.

Cardiovascular Disease Manifestations

Cardiovascular diseases present with distinct clinical signs that are crucial for prompt diagnosis and management. Recognizing these signs helps to prevent further complications such as heart attacks or strokes.

- Chest Pain (Angina): One of the most recognized symptoms of cardiovascular disease, angina is caused by myocardial ischemia. The pathophysiology involves an imbalance between the heart's oxygen supply and demand, often due to coronary artery disease.

- Edema: Fluid retention, particularly in the lower extremities (peripheral edema) or lungs (pulmonary edema), is a common sign of heart failure. This results from the heart's inability to pump efficiently, leading to fluid accumulation in tissues.

- Palpitations: A sensation of irregular or rapid heartbeats, palpitations can occur in arrhythmias like atrial fibrillation or ventricular tachycardia. These abnormalities in heart rhythm are often due to electrical disturbances within the heart's conduction system.

By understanding the underlying pathophysiology, healthcare providers can associate clinical signs with specific cardiovascular conditions. For example, chest pain that radiates to the left arm or jaw, accompanied by diaphoresis (sweating) and dyspnea, is highly suggestive of myocardial infarction (heart attack), prompting urgent intervention.

Gastrointestinal Disease Signs

The gastrointestinal system manifests a wide array of clinical signs depending on the underlying pathology. These signs are key to identifying disorders such as gastritis, inflammatory bowel disease (IBD), or liver disease.

- Abdominal Pain: The nature and location of abdominal pain often provide clues to its cause. For instance, right upper quadrant pain may indicate gallbladder disease, while left lower quadrant pain suggests diverticulitis. The pathophysiology of pain varies—whether it stems from inflammation, obstruction, or ischemia.

- Jaundice: A yellow discoloration of the skin and eyes, jaundice results from elevated bilirubin levels, often due to liver dysfunction or bile duct obstruction. Hepatitis, cirrhosis, and gallstones are common causes.

- Diarrhea: Frequent loose stools may be seen in conditions like gastroenteritis, IBD, or malabsorption syndromes. The pathophysiology involves increased intestinal motility, inflammation, or impaired nutrient absorption.

Understanding these manifestations within the context of clinical pathophysiology allows providers to identify the cause and severity of gastrointestinal issues. For example, jaundice with abdominal pain and weight loss might indicate pancreatic cancer, while diarrhea with blood and mucus suggests inflammatory bowel disease.

Neurological and Musculoskeletal Signs

Neurological and musculoskeletal diseases often present with specific clinical signs that reflect underlying pathophysiological changes in the nervous or muscular systems.

- Weakness or Paralysis: Weakness can occur in conditions like stroke, multiple sclerosis, or muscular dystrophy. The pathophysiology may involve ischemic damage to brain tissue (as in stroke) or demyelination of nerves (as in multiple sclerosis).
- Tremors: Involuntary shaking movements, tremors are often seen in neurological disorders such as Parkinson's disease. These result from dysfunction in the basal ganglia, a brain region involved in motor control.
- Joint Pain (Arthralgia): In conditions like rheumatoid arthritis, joint pain and swelling are caused by chronic inflammation of the synovial membrane, leading to joint destruction over time.
- Recognizing neurological and musculoskeletal signs is critical for early diagnosis and intervention. For instance, a sudden onset of weakness in one side of the body, slurred speech, and

difficulty walking suggests a stroke, requiring immediate medical attention.

Linking Clinical Signs to Disease Processes

To make informed clinical decisions, healthcare providers must not only recognize these signs but also connect them to underlying disease processes. This requires a deep understanding of pathophysiology, as the same sign can be caused by different conditions. For example, dyspnea can result from both respiratory (asthma, COPD) and cardiovascular (heart failure, pulmonary embolism) diseases. By integrating clinical signs with the pathophysiology of the disease, healthcare providers can narrow down potential diagnoses and initiate the appropriate diagnostic tests and treatments.

Clinical Case Example

Consider a patient who presents with chest pain, shortness of breath, and diaphoresis. Vital signs show tachycardia, hypotension, and low oxygen saturation. An ECG reveals ST-segment elevation. These clinical signs strongly suggest an acute myocardial infarction (heart attack), with the underlying pathophysiology involving the blockage of a coronary artery, leading to ischemia and infarction of heart tissue. Immediate intervention with reperfusion therapy (e.g., angioplasty) is necessary to restore blood flow and prevent further tissue damage.

MODULE THREE

LESSON: X-RAY INTERPRETATION; SPOTTING PATHOPHYSIOLOGICAL CHANGES

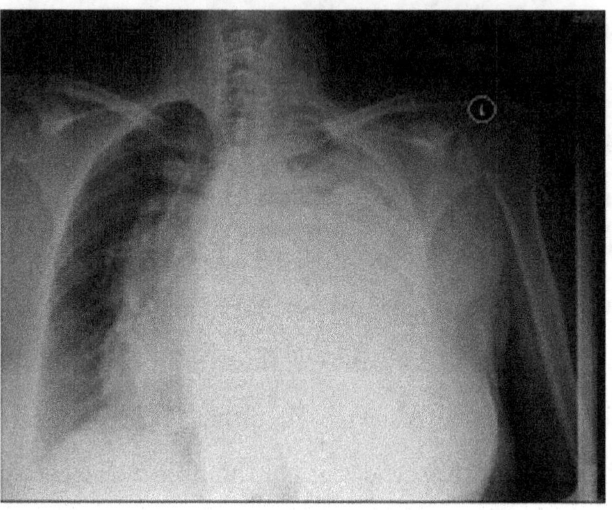

X-rays are among the most commonly used imaging tools in healthcare. For healthcare providers, understanding how to interpret X-ray images is vital in diagnosing various diseases, especially in the respiratory and musculoskeletal systems. In this lesson, we will explore the basics of X-ray interpretation, focusing on identifying key pathophysiological changes in the body.

Principles of X-ray Imaging

X-rays utilize electromagnetic radiation to create images of the internal structures of the body. When X-rays pass through the body, they are absorbed by different tissues at varying levels, resulting in images where denser structures, like bones, appear white, while air-filled spaces, such as the lungs, appear black. Soft tissues fall somewhere in between on the grayscale.

Understanding this principle is crucial for interpreting X-rays. Dense materials like bones absorb more X-rays, creating more opaque areas (whiter on the image), while less dense structures, like air-filled lungs, allow more X-rays to pass through, appearing darker. Fluids, like blood or pleural effusion, will appear more opaque than air but less than bone.

The ABCDE Approach to Chest X-rays

A systematic approach is critical when reviewing X-rays, particularly chest X-rays (CXR), to avoid missing important findings. The ABCDE approach is commonly used to ensure a thorough assessment:

- A - Airway: Start by assessing the trachea and bronchi. The trachea should be centrally located. Any deviation may suggest conditions like a pneumothorax, pleural effusion, or mass effect from a tumor.
- B - Breathing (Lungs): Look at the lung fields for symmetry. The lungs should appear dark because they are filled with air. Look for areas of increased opacity (white spots), which could indicate consolidation (as in pneumonia), pulmonary edema, or atelectasis (collapsed lung).
- C - Circulation (Heart and Blood Vessels): The heart size should occupy less than 50% of the thoracic width in a normal

chest X-ray. An enlarged heart (cardiomegaly) may indicate heart failure. Assess the blood vessels for any abnormalities, such as widened mediastinum, which could suggest aortic dissection.

- D - Diaphragm: The diaphragm should appear smooth and dome-shaped. A raised diaphragm can indicate phrenic nerve injury, while a flattened diaphragm is seen in conditions like chronic obstructive pulmonary disease (COPD). Free air under the diaphragm is a sign of pneumoperitoneum, indicating perforation of a hollow organ.

- E - Everything Else: Finally, review the bones (ribs, clavicles, vertebrae) for fractures or abnormalities. Also, assess the soft tissues for any masses, foreign objects, or abnormalities.

This systematic method ensures that every relevant area is thoroughly checked, reducing the chances of overlooking critical signs of disease.

Recognizing Pathological Patterns on X-rays

X-rays can reveal characteristic patterns that correspond to different diseases. Recognizing these patterns can help healthcare providers identify the underlying pathophysiological changes and diagnose conditions accurately.

- Pneumonia (Consolidation): Pneumonia typically appears as an area of increased opacity (whiteness) in the lung fields, representing consolidation due to infection. The borders of the consolidation may be well-defined or patchy, depending on the extent and type of pneumonia. A "lobar" pattern of consolidation is often seen in bacterial pneumonia, while viral pneumonia may present with a more diffuse or interstitial pattern.

- Pleural Effusion: Pleural effusion, the accumulation of fluid in the pleural space, appears as a homogeneous opacity in the lower lung zones. It typically causes a "blunting" of the costophrenic angle (the angle where the diaphragm meets the chest wall). In more significant effusions, the fluid may shift the trachea or mediastinum to the opposite side.

- Pneumothorax: Pneumothorax, or collapsed lung, appears as a lack of lung markings in the affected area. The lung may appear more radiolucent (darker), and the edge of the collapsed lung may be visible as a thin white line. A tension pneumothorax, a life-threatening condition, causes the trachea to deviate away from the affected side due to increased pressure.

- Pulmonary Edema: Seen in conditions like heart failure, pulmonary edema manifests as "batwing" or "butterfly" opacities, representing fluid accumulation in the lungs. This pattern is often accompanied by an enlarged heart and engorged pulmonary vessels.

- Chronic Obstructive Pulmonary Disease (COPD): In patients with COPD, X-rays often reveal hyperinflated lungs with flattened diaphragms. The lung fields appear darker due to the increased air trapping, and the heart may appear elongated and narrow due to the expanded lungs.

Musculoskeletal Findings on X-rays

While chest X-rays are primarily used for assessing respiratory and cardiovascular conditions, X-rays are also vital in diagnosing musculoskeletal issues. Bone fractures, dislocations, and degenerative diseases can be identified through careful examination of the skeletal structures.

- Fractures: Fractures appear as disruptions in the normal continuity of the bone. They can range from simple, linear fractures to complex, comminuted fractures where the bone is broken into multiple pieces. Stress fractures may be subtler, often presenting as faint lines of radiolucency.

- Osteoarthritis: In cases of osteoarthritis, X-rays reveal joint space narrowing, subchondral sclerosis (increased bone density beneath the cartilage), and osteophytes (bone spurs). These findings reflect the degenerative nature of the disease, where cartilage breakdown leads to joint pain and stiffness.

- Rheumatoid Arthritis: Unlike osteoarthritis, which affects weight-bearing joints, rheumatoid arthritis often affects smaller joints like those in the hands and feet. X-rays may show joint erosion, soft tissue swelling, and, in later stages, joint deformity and ankylosis (fusion of the joint).

Common Pitfalls in X-ray Interpretation

Even experienced healthcare providers can sometimes misinterpret X-rays due to common pitfalls. Recognizing these potential errors can help improve accuracy in diagnosis:

- Overlapping Structures: Sometimes normal structures overlap in ways that mimic pathology. For instance, the shadow of the scapula can be mistaken for a lung mass. Always consider anatomical relationships when interpreting images.

- Underexposure/Overexposure: The quality of the X-ray image depends on the exposure settings. Underexposed images may make it difficult to see important details, while overexposed images can obscure abnormalities. Always ensure that the exposure is adequate for a detailed review.

- Misinterpretation of Normal Variants: Some normal anatomical variations can be mistaken for pathology. For example, a prominent thymus gland in a child may appear as a mediastinal mass. Familiarity with normal variants is essential to avoid unnecessary concern.

Clinical Relevance: Linking X-ray Findings to Pathophysiology

To make accurate clinical decisions, healthcare providers must link the findings on X-rays to the underlying pathophysiology of the disease. For example, in a patient with pneumonia, the consolidation seen on the X-ray corresponds to the inflammatory process in the alveoli, where infection leads to the accumulation of pus and fluid.

Similarly, in a patient with heart failure, the pulmonary edema observed on the X-ray reflects increased pressure in the pulmonary circulation due to the heart's inability to pump effectively.

Incorporating clinical signs and symptoms with X-ray findings allows for a more comprehensive understanding of the disease process. For example, a patient presenting with fever, productive cough, and shortness of breath, along with an X-ray showing consolidation, is likely suffering from bacterial pneumonia, and treatment should be initiated promptly.

Clinical Case Example

A 65-year-old man presents to the emergency department with shortness of breath and fatigue. On examination, his vital signs reveal tachycardia and low oxygen saturation. A chest X-ray shows bilateral fluffy opacities consistent with pulmonary edema, and the heart size is markedly enlarged, suggesting heart failure. The pathophysiology behind these findings involves the heart's inability to pump blood efficiently, leading to fluid accumulation in the lungs. This patient's X-ray findings, combined with his clinical symptoms, confirm the diagnosis of heart failure, and treatment with diuretics and vasodilators is initiated.

MODULE FOUR

LESSON: CLINICAL MANIFESTATIONS OF COMMON DISEASES

Understanding the clinical manifestations of diseases is vital for healthcare providers to identify and manage conditions effectively. This lesson delves into the most common diseases encountered in clinical practice, exploring how their underlying pathophysiology translates into specific signs and symptoms. The focus will be on linking these manifestations to the mechanisms driving the disease processes.

Respiratory Diseases

Respiratory diseases often present with a range of symptoms due to impaired gas exchange, airway obstruction, or inflammation in the respiratory tract. The clinical manifestations are diverse but share common features that reflect the underlying pathophysiological changes.

- Asthma: Asthma is a chronic inflammatory disease of the airways, characterized by episodic airflow obstruction. The hallmark symptoms of asthma include wheezing, shortness of breath, chest tightness, and coughing, particularly at night or early in the morning. Pathophysiologically, asthma involves hyper-responsiveness of the airways to various triggers such as allergens, exercise, or cold air. During an asthma attack, bronchoconstriction, mucus hypersecretion, and airway inflammation lead to reduced airflow, manifesting as the clinical symptoms described.

- Chronic Obstructive Pulmonary Disease (COPD): COPD encompasses two primary conditions: emphysema and chronic bronchitis. In emphysema, the destruction of alveolar walls leads to reduced surface area for gas exchange, while in chronic bronchitis, excessive mucus production causes airway obstruction. Patients with COPD often present with chronic cough, sputum production, and dyspnea. The characteristic "barrel chest" appearance, seen in advanced COPD, results from hyperinflation of the lungs due to air trapping. Over time, patients develop hypoxemia and hypercapnia due to inefficient gas exchange, contributing to symptoms of fatigue and decreased exercise tolerance.

- Pneumonia: Pneumonia, an infection of the lungs, presents with fever, productive cough, pleuritic chest pain, and shortness of breath. The pathophysiology of pneumonia involves the accumulation of inflammatory exudate in the alveoli, impairing oxygen exchange. Depending on the pathogen, pneumonia can cause different patterns on imaging and clinical presentation. Bacterial pneumonia tends to produce localized consolidation, while viral or atypical pneumonia may present with a more diffuse pattern of lung involvement.

Cardiovascular Diseases

Cardiovascular diseases often manifest as chest pain, dyspnea, palpitations, and fatigue, reflecting the heart's role in maintaining circulation. Early recognition of these symptoms is critical for preventing complications like heart attacks or strokes.

- Myocardial Infarction (Heart Attack): Myocardial infarction occurs when there is a sudden blockage of blood flow to a part of the heart muscle, usually due to a thrombus in the coronary artery. The classic presentation is severe, crushing chest pain that radiates to the left arm, neck, or jaw, accompanied by sweating, nausea, and shortness of breath. The underlying pathophysiology involves ischemia and subsequent necrosis of heart tissue, leading to impaired contractile function. If untreated, this can result in arrhythmias, heart failure, or cardiogenic shock.

- Congestive Heart Failure (CHF): CHF is the inability of the heart to pump effectively, leading to inadequate circulation of blood to meet the body's needs. Clinical manifestations include shortness of breath, fatigue, peripheral edema, and orthopnea (difficulty breathing while lying flat). In left-sided heart failure, fluid backs up into the lungs, causing pulmonary edema and breathlessness. In right-sided heart failure, fluid accumulates in the body, causing peripheral edema, hepatomegaly (enlarged liver), and jugular venous distension. The pathophysiology of heart failure involves a combination of reduced cardiac output and compensatory mechanisms, such as activation of the renin-angiotensin-aldosterone system (RAAS), which further exacerbates fluid retention.

- Hypertension: Hypertension, or high blood pressure, is often asymptomatic in its early stages, earning it the nickname "the silent killer." Over time, chronic hypertension damages the blood vessels, leading to complications such as stroke, myocardial infarction, heart failure, and kidney disease. Patients may present with headache, dizziness, or visual disturbances in more advanced cases. Pathophysiologically, hypertension involves increased peripheral resistance, which places extra strain on the heart and blood vessels, causing damage over time.

Gastrointestinal Diseases

Gastrointestinal (GI) diseases can present with a wide array of symptoms, including abdominal pain, vomiting, diarrhea, and gastrointestinal bleeding. Understanding the clinical manifestations of these conditions is key to prompt diagnosis and treatment.

- Gastritis and Peptic Ulcer Disease: Gastritis refers to inflammation of the stomach lining, while peptic ulcers are open sores that develop on the inner lining of the stomach or duodenum. Common symptoms include epigastric pain (pain in the upper abdomen), nausea, vomiting, and bloating. In peptic ulcer disease, the pain is often described as burning or gnawing and may improve with eating or antacids. The pathophysiology involves the breakdown of the protective mucosal barrier, often due to Helicobacter pylori infection or prolonged use of nonsteroidal anti-inflammatory drugs (NSAIDs), leading to increased gastric acid secretion and mucosal damage.

- Irritable Bowel Syndrome (IBS): IBS is a functional disorder characterized by chronic abdominal pain, bloating, and altered bowel habits (diarrhea, constipation, or both). The exact pathophysiology of IBS is unclear, but it is thought to involve abnormal motility, visceral hypersensitivity, and psychological factors. Patients often report symptoms that fluctuate in intensity and are triggered by stress or certain foods.

- Liver Disease (Cirrhosis): Cirrhosis, the advanced stage of liver fibrosis, results from chronic liver damage due to conditions like viral hepatitis, alcohol abuse, or non-alcoholic fatty liver disease. Clinical manifestations include jaundice (yellowing of the skin and eyes), ascites (fluid accumulation in the abdomen), variceal bleeding, and hepatic encephalopathy (confusion or altered mental status due to liver failure). The pathophysiology involves the replacement of healthy liver tissue with scar tissue, which impairs liver function and disrupts blood flow through the organ.

Neurological Diseases

Neurological diseases can lead to a range of symptoms depending on which part of the nervous system is affected. Early recognition of these signs is crucial for preventing long-term disability.

- Stroke (Cerebrovascular Accident): A stroke occurs when blood flow to a part of the brain is interrupted, either by a clot (ischemic stroke) or bleeding (hemorrhagic stroke). The clinical presentation includes sudden onset of weakness or paralysis on one side of the body, difficulty speaking (aphasia), facial drooping, and loss of coordination. The pathophysiology of stroke involves ischemia or hemorrhage leading to brain cell death. Rapid treatment is critical to minimize brain damage and improve outcomes.

- Parkinson's Disease: Parkinson's disease is a neurodegenerative disorder characterized by tremors, bradykinesia (slowness of movement), muscle rigidity, and postural instability. These symptoms result from the loss of dopamine-producing neurons in the substantia nigra, a part of the brain involved in motor control. As dopamine levels decrease, patients develop the characteristic movement difficulties associated with the disease.

- Multiple Sclerosis (MS): MS is an autoimmune disease in which the immune system attacks the protective myelin sheath covering nerve fibers, leading to disrupted communication between the brain and the rest of the body. Clinical manifestations of MS include fatigue, numbness, weakness, difficulty walking, and visual disturbances. The pathophysiology involves demyelination of nerve fibers and the formation of scar tissue (sclerosis), which interferes with nerve conduction.

Endocrine and Metabolic Diseases

Endocrine disorders often present with systemic symptoms due to hormonal imbalances. Metabolic diseases like diabetes can have far-reaching effects on multiple organ systems.

- Diabetes Mellitus (Type 1 and Type 2): Diabetes is characterized by chronic hyperglycemia (high blood sugar levels) due to insufficient insulin production (Type 1) or insulin resistance (Type 2). Common symptoms include increased thirst (polydipsia), frequent urination (polyuria), weight loss, and fatigue. Over time, uncontrolled diabetes can lead to complications such as retinopathy (eye damage), nephropathy (kidney damage), neuropathy (nerve damage), and cardiovascular disease. The pathophysiology of Type 1 diabetes involves autoimmune destruction of insulin-producing beta cells in the pancreas, while Type 2 diabetes is linked to insulin resistance in peripheral tissues.

- Hypothyroidism: Hypothyroidism occurs when the thyroid gland fails to produce sufficient thyroid hormones, leading to a slowing of metabolic processes. Clinical manifestations include fatigue, weight gain, cold intolerance, dry skin, and constipation. The pathophysiology involves decreased levels of thyroid hormones (T3 and T4), which slows the body's metabolism and affects various organ systems.

CONCLUSION

Clinical pathophysiology is more than just the study of disease processes; it is a roadmap that guides every step of patient care, from diagnosis to treatment and recovery. By integrating pathophysiological insights into their practice, healthcare providers can enhance their ability to provide high-quality, evidence-based care that truly makes a difference in patients' lives. This book is a resource for ongoing learning, one that supports healthcare professionals in making well-informed, confident clinical decisions.

The aim of this book has been to bridge the gap between theory and practice, empowering healthcare providers, respiratory therapists, nurses, and doctors alike—to not only recognize the clinical manifestations of disease but also understand the physiological and pathological processes behind them.

As you move forward in your practice, continue to embrace the critical thinking and deep understanding that pathophysiology offers. By doing so, you will not only enhance your skills but also contribute to the health and well-being of those you serve.

<u>REFERENCES</u>

Abraham, W. T., & Adamson, P. B. (2016). *"Heart Failure: Pathophysiology, Diagnosis, and Treatment."* Journal of the American College of Cardiology.

Bhatt, D. L., & Steg, P. G. (2017). *"Management of Myocardial Infarction."* The Lancet.

Boyle, J. P., Thompson, T. J., & Gregg, E. W. (2010). *"Global Prevalence of Diabetes and its Complications."* Diabetes Care.

Brooks, D. & Tipping, N. (2015). *"Chronic Obstructive Pulmonary Disease: Mechanisms and Management."* Thorax.

Davis, B. R., & Cutler, J. A. (2015). *"Hypertension and Cardiovascular Disease."* The New England Journal of Medicine.

Goldstein, L. B., & Simel, D. L. (2018). *"Clinical Diagnosis of Stroke."* JAMA.

Hall, J. E. (2016). Guyton and Hall Textbook of Medical Physiology. Elsevier.

Horne, B. D., & Anderson, J. L. (2019). *"Pathophysiology of Heart Failure and Its Clinical Manifestations."* Circulation.

Huppmann, A. R., & Brown, D. L. (2017). *"Pathogenesis and Clinical Manifestations of Pneumonia."* Journal of Respiratory Diseases.

Jain, V., & Agarwal, S. (2017). *"Imaging in Respiratory Diseases: The Role of X-rays."* Journal of Clinical Radiology.

www.ingramcontent.com/pod-product-compliance
Lightning Source LLC
Chambersburg PA
CBHW061327140726

47998CB00007B/2584